Why
do people commit
crime?

olf

HODDER
Wayland

an imprint of Hodder Children's Books

© 2004 White-Thomson Publishing Ltd
Produced for Hodder Wayland by
White-Thomson Publishing Ltd
2/3 St Andrew's Place, Lewes BN7 1UP

Other titles in this series:
Why are people racist?
Why are people refugees?
Why are people terrorists?
Why are people vegetarian?
Why do families break up?
Why do people abuse human rights?
Why do people bully?
Why do people drink alcohol?
Why do people fight wars?
Why do people gamble?
Why do people harm animals?
Why do people join gangs?
Why do people live on the streets?
Why do people smoke?
Why do people take drugs?

For more information on this series and
other Hodder Wayland titles, go to
www.hodderwayland.co.uk

Editor: Philip de Ste. Croix
Cover design: Hodder Children's Books
Inside design: Malcolm Walker
Consultant: Professor Mike Hough, Director,
        Criminal Policy Research Unit, South Bank
        University, London
Picture research: Shelley Noronha, Glass Onion
Indexer: Amanda O'Neill

Published in Great Britain in 2004 by Hodder
Wayland, an imprint of Hodder Children's Books

This paperback edition published in 2006

The right of Alex Woolf to be identified as the
author has been asserted by him in accordance
with the Copyright, Designs and Patents Act 1988.

Every effort has been made to trace copyright
holders. However, the publishers apologise for any
unintentional omissions and would be pleased in
such cases to add an acknowledgement in any
future editions.

British Library Cataloguing in Publication Data
Woolf, Alex
   Why do people commit crime?
   1. Crime - Juvenile literature 2. Criminal
   Psychology - Juvenile literature
   I. Title
   364.2

ISBN 0 7502 4828 9

Printed by C&C Offset, China

Hodder Children's Books
A division of Hodder Headline Limited
338 Euston Road, London NW1 3BH

Picture acknowledgements
The publisher would like to thank the following
for their kind permission to use their pictures:
AKG London 6 (Erich Lessing), 7, 36 (Gilles
Mermet); Corbis (cover), 12 (David Turnley), 28;
Eye Ubiquitous 8 (Sue Passmore); Hodder Wayland
Picture Library 44; Mary Evans Picture Library 37;
Popperfoto/Reuters (contents) (left), (contents)
(right) (Eric Gaillard), 5 (Jonathan Drake), 10 (Fred
Prouser), 13, 15 (Eric Gaillard), 16, 17 (Sam
Mircovich), 18 (China Photo), 21 (Colin Braley), 24,
25 (Timothy A. Clary), 26, 32 (Faisal Mahmood), 33
(Wilfredo Lee), 34 (Jim Bourg), 38 (Sergio
Barzaghi), 40 (Federal Bureau of Prisons), 41
(Steven M. Falk), 43; Rex Features (imprint page)
(David Browne), 4, 9 (Sipa/Roger Wilson), 23
(DMI/Mirek Towski), 30 (Des Jenson), 35 (Kevin
Wisniewski), 42 (David Browne); Topham/AP 22;
Topham/ImageWorks 11 (Bob Daemmrich), 14
(Bob Daemmrich), 20, 27 (Larry Kolvoord), 29
(David Lassman), 31 (Bob Daemmrich), 39 (Jack
Kurtz); Topham Picturepoint 19; WTPix 45.

Cover picture: Hands of a prisoner on cell bars.

Contents

1.What is crime?

Why do we need laws?

A crime is any act that breaks the law. Laws are sets of rules that everyone in a country must abide by. Countries need laws. Without them, life would be very uncertain and dangerous. People could drive at whatever speed they liked. They could steal, or even kill, and no one would be able to stop them. Laws are needed to maintain order, and to protect people and property.

In a democracy – a country in which the people elect their own government – the population have some control over the laws that are passed. In non-democratic countries governments can pass whatever laws they like, and a crime is whatever the government says it is.

◀ A coffee shop in Holland. In these places it is legal to sell and use small amounts of cannabis. In Britain, it is illegal to sell cannabis, although the use of small amounts is tolerated. In the USA both using and selling this drug is against the law.

◀ In Singapore, a group of women on their day off watch two policemen patrolling the park. It is illegal to smoke in public places in Singapore, and those caught littering are sometimes made to clean the streets.

For example, in Singapore the government has made it a crime to buy and sell bubble gum, and you can even be fined for not flushing the toilet.

The laws of a country are based on its beliefs about right and wrong. Some laws are common to all countries. For instance, everyone knows that murder and theft are wrong, and every country has laws against them, although the meanings of these crimes can vary from country to country. As well as these common crimes, there are other types of activity, such as drug use, gambling, and prostitution, that are crimes in some countries, but not in others.

FACT:
The following figures were taken from a survey carried out in 23 countries in Europe and North America in 2000. They show the number of people per 100 of the population who suffered from a particular crime in the previous year:

Burglary (breaking into a property to steal)	1.8
Car theft	1.0
Personal theft	3.9
Robbery (theft with violence or threat)	0.8
Sexual assault	1.7
Violent assault	3.5

International Crime Victim Surveys

The history of crime

Crime has existed ever since laws were introduced. The first collection of laws, known as the Code of Hammurabi, was developed in the eighteenth century BC. Other codes of law were created by the ancient Hebrews, Greeks and Romans. From these it is possible to work out the sorts of crime that were committed in ancient times.

◀ *This ancient Egyptian wallpainting shows a slave being beaten by his master, possibly for disobedience. Beatings were the most common punishment in ancient Egypt.*

Murder and theft were common to all cultures. Treason, or betrayal of one's tribe or country, was another act viewed by all ancient peoples as a crime. As civilization developed, new inventions arose, such as books and money. This in turn led to new crimes. The Romans found it necessary to pass laws against actions such as libel (a false statement that damages someone's reputation), perjury (lying under oath), and bribery.

▶ *An illustration of witches from a fifteenth-century French book. During the Middle Ages, witchcraft was regarded as a crime and witches were put to death.*

The nature of crime has altered through history reflecting the concerns of each age, and changes in the opportunities for committing crime. During the Middle Ages, when the Church was very powerful in Europe, it was a crime to hold religious beliefs that were different from those of the Church.

> The criminals of sixteenth-century London were very well-organized. They even arranged training for new recruits: 'There was a school house set up to learn [teach] young boys to cut purses. There were hung up … a pocket…. The pocket had in it certain counters and was hung about with hawk's bells … and he that could take out a counter without any noise was allowed to be a Public Foister [pickpocket].'
>
> *William Fleetwood, Recorder of London, 1585*

By the eighteenth century, due to population growth and increasing divisions between rich and poor, there was a rise in crimes against property. These included poaching, smuggling and highway robbery.

Crime in the modern world

In the twentieth century, the face of crime changed again, partly because of advances in technology. The invention of the car meant that traffic laws and laws against reckless or drunken driving had to be introduced.

The use of personal computers and the Internet in the 1980s and 1990s created new types of crime, including hacking (accessing files held on someone else's computer without their permission), and spreading computer viruses that can destroy files. Another common crime today is computer fraud. This means cheating people out of money or goods – for example by using someone else's credit card details to buy something on the Internet.

▲ *Cyberstalking – sending someone threatening or abusive emails – is a new crime of the Internet age. In 1999 the first person to be found guilty of cyberstalking was sentenced to six years in prison.*

The growth of business and industry is behind a rise in 'white-collar' crime. White-collar crime is crime committed by professional people at their jobs. White-collar crimes include stealing money from an employer's bank account (as opposed to robbing the cash register), cheating customers, evading tax, and engaging in bribery. The overall cost of white-collar crime is thought to be much greater than the combined cost of burglary, car theft and robbery.

FACT:

During the nineteenth century, the western United States experienced a rapid population growth. Because the region was so huge with large distances between towns, law enforcement was very difficult, and crime flourished. Crimes included horse theft, cattle rustling (stealing), bank robberies, and the holding up of stagecoaches (horse-drawn coaches). This time period is often made to look fun and exciting in movies and books, but the Wild West, as it came to be known, was a violent place, and murder was common. Feuding cattlemen often sorted out their differences in a gunfight.

As we move into the twenty-first century, most of the motives that lie behind crime, like greed and hatred, remain the same. Only the methods have changed. New crimes will certainly emerge, reflecting the concerns of the time. Perhaps pollution, the non-recycling of rubbish, and cruelty to animals will be the crimes of the future.

weblinks

For more information about people's experience of crime, the police, and justice systems, go to www.waylinks.co.uk/series/why/crime

◀ *Sometimes law and order can break down when a community feels under threat. Anger at police racism led black Americans to riot in the streets of Los Angeles in April 1992.*

2. Why do people break the law?

Is there a criminal type?

People commit crimes for many reasons. A murderer may be provoked by anger or hatred, while a drug-dealer is driven by a desire to make money. Because there are so many different kinds of crime, and so many reasons for it, the people who commit crimes do not fit into a particular type. They can be rich or poor, male or female, and of any ethnic background.

This does not explain why most people live law-abiding lives, while a minority commit crime. Some people argue it is because certain people have been born with a personality that leads them into criminal behaviour. It may be that they are impulsive, self-centred people who enjoy taking risks.

◀ Some people may commit crimes for the sheer thrill of breaking the law. Hollywood star Winona Ryder, shown here arriving at court, was found guilty in November 2002 of shoplifting goods from a Los Angeles store.

◀ *Some people argue that if children see violence on television, they are more likely to behave violently.*

In the case of violent criminals it could be that they have damaged personalities, perhaps due to bad experiences in childhood. This may make them unstable, aggressive, and less able to control their actions.

Others believe that people are not born criminals, but are influenced by their family, friends and environment to break the law. If children see people around them committing crimes and getting away with it, they are tempted to try the same thing themselves. On the other hand, people who see that good behaviour earns rewards, and are taught early on about the differences between right and wrong, may be less prone to criminal behaviour in later life.

> 'Negligent [careless] parenting is undoubtedly a contributing factor [to crime] and, along with other factors such as truancy, lack of discipline in schools, drugs, pornography, a material-obsessed media, and the lack of religion as a framework for the teaching of right and wrong, works to increase the chances of children, especially boys, stumbling into crime.'
>
> *Shelagh Shepherd, British journalist, May 2002*

Is society to blame?

While some blame individuals for crime, others blame society. They claim that crime is caused by poverty and inequality. There is evidence to support this view. Both rich and poor people commit crimes, but crime rates tend to be higher in poorer communities, especially those located in inner cities.

Why is this? One explanation has been put forward, known as 'strain theory'. In most cultures, people generally work to earn money so they can afford a comfortable lifestyle. People with high-paying jobs can buy a nice house, a car and good clothes, and so there is less pressure on them to find other ways of getting those things.

> **FACT**
> During 2000 in the USA, about 5.5 per cent of city inhabitants (i.e. between five and six people for every 100 living there) committed at least one crime, compared to around 4 per cent of people who lived in the suburbs or in the country.
> *FBI Uniform Crime Reports*

◀ In today's cities, the wealth on display can tempt some people into crime. Some of the very poorest may feel that they have to steal to feed themselves and their families.

According to strain theory, poorer people who cannot afford the house, car and nice clothing, can react in several ways. Some may try to achieve these goals through hard work. Others may decide to forget these goals as an impossible dream, and aim simply to enjoy a reasonable standard of living. People who make either of these choices will not turn to crime.

Other reactions though are likely to lead people to commit crime. Some people wish to achieve these goals, but they know they never can do so on what they earn. So, they find other ways. They may steal from their job, or turn to gambling, prostitution or theft. Other people reject these goals and also reject the idea of working for a living. They must find other ways of supporting themselves. In some cases this can lead them to crime. Both rich and poor people can make these choices, but there is more pressure on poorer people to act in this way.

▲ *Gamblers in Lima, Peru play the slot machines. People who become addicted to gambling can sometimes turn to crime to fund their habIt.*

Young criminals

Since the 1950s, there has been a steep rise in crimes committed by young people. Increases were especially rapid during the 1980s and 1990s (see fact box). Nowadays, more than a third of all crimes are committed by people under eighteen. Typical crimes of young people include shoplifting, vandalism, joyriding (stealing cars and driving them around), and drug use.

One reason for this is that people living in inner cities are getting poorer. Young people growing up in these places lack opportunities for education and employment, and so they may turn to crime. Some join gangs, often associated with a kind of music they like. As members of a gang, young people enjoy a sense of belonging that they lack in ordinary life. Gang members sometimes put pressure on each other to act in dangerous or illegal ways. They might get into fights or damage property.

In some countries, immigration can be a strong factor in youth crime. People arriving from abroad often struggle to find jobs, because they do not speak the language very well or do not understand the culture. They may also face discrimination. Some turn to crime simply to survive.

weblinks

For more information about street gangs, go to www.waylinks.co.uk/series/why/crime

▼ *A member of a street gang from Texas. According to a 1997 report from the US National Gang Crime Research Center, over half of gang members have committed crimes for financial gain.*

France and Germany, for example, have experienced a rise in drug dealing and gun use since the early 1990s, when thousands of young people crossed the borders from eastern to western Europe. Of course not all people growing up under these conditions become criminals. Many people use difficult beginnings as motivation to achieve great things. Still others find it important to try and find ways to prevent crimes in the kinds of neighbourhoods in which they grew up.

▲ *Some football fans can turn violent, especially after they have been drinking alcohol. Here, Tunisian and English supporters clash in Marseilles, France, during the 1998 World Cup.*

FACT:

This table shows that over a ten-year period between the mid-1980s and mid-1990s there was an increase in violent crime committed by young people in the countries sampled.

Country	Year	Age Group	Number of young people arrested (for each 100,000)
England/Wales	1986	14-16	360
	1994		580
USA	1984	10-17	300
	1994		500
West Germany	1984	14-18	300
	1995		760

Why do people commit murder?

Murder is considered the most serious of all crimes. It is defined as the deliberate and unjustified killing of one person by another. In law, murder means killing someone deliberately, unlike manslaughter, which means causing death without having the previous intention to do so. Killing in war or in self-defence is not usually regarded as murder.

People commit murder for many reasons, most often for gain. A robber may murder someone to get their money, for example. Murders are also committed out of passion – because of jealousy, anger or a desire for revenge. In fact, many murders are committed by people who know the victim. In the USA around 21 per cent of murdered women are killed by someone they know.

◀ *On 20 April 1999, fearful students wait outside Columbine High School in Denver, USA, where two teenagers went on the rampage, killing twelve students and a teacher before committing suicide.*

case study · case study · case study · case study · case study

Thomas Hamilton was sacked from his job as a scoutmaster in 1974, and had nursed a grudge against society ever since. On 13 March 1996, Hamilton entered a primary school in the Scottish town of Dunblane, armed with four handguns. He made his way to the gym hall and opened fire on a class full of four- and five-year-olds. He killed sixteen children and their teacher, Gwen Mayor. Ten children and two adults were also wounded in the attack. Hamilton then shot and killed himself. In the public enquiry that followed, evidence emerged of Hamilton's unbalanced state of mind.

People may also commit murders because they are mentally ill. This has often been given as an explanation for serial killers – people who kill several times. Peter Sutcliffe, who murdered 13 women in the 1970s, claimed to have heard voices telling him to kill prostitutes. Similarly, Jeffrey Dahmer, who murdered 17 young men during the 1980s, showed clear signs of mental illness.

▲ *Murder trials like the one involving O.J. Simpson (above) are always given plenty of coverage in the media, because they make dramatic news stories. This may make people think that murder is a more common crime than it is.*

Despite the intense media interest in murder cases, violent crimes only make up around 20 per cent of all reported crime incidents, and only a very small proportion of these result in the death of the victim. Murder rates rose by about two or three times in North America and Europe between the 1950s and 1990s, but have stabilized in recent years. Murder remains a relatively rare crime.

3. What is organized crime?

Criminal gangs

Some people work together in illegal ways in order to make money. By combining their skills with others they are able to commit more ambitious crimes than they could if they were acting alone. This kind of activity is known as 'organized crime'.

weblinks

For more information about the history and activities of organized crime, go to www.waylinks.co.uk/series/why/crime

Some of these criminal groups form powerful gangs. They may operate rather like a legitimate business, with bosses and employees with different levels of responsibility. However, they make their money by trading in illegal products, such as drugs, gambling, prostitution and pornography. They also earn money from loansharking, which means lending money at very high rates of interest and threatening physical harm if the money isn't repaid. Another method is to demand money from small businesses in return for not damaging their property. This is known as a protection racket.

▲ A member of the Triad, a Chinese organized crime gang, is sentenced to death in a Chinese court in Chengdu in April 2001.

Crime gangs are ruthless organizations that use violence and intimidation to survive. They evade the law by bribing officials and by acting in secret, often using a legitimate business as a cover for their illegal activities. The most famous organized crime group is the Mafia. This is a loose network of crime families that originally came from Sicily, and started to operate in the USA around 1900. They were heavily involved in alcohol trading during the period of Prohibition (1920-1933) when alcohol was banned in the USA. Since then the American mafia has profited from gambling, loansharking, prostitution and drugs.

▲ *The 1969 trial of sixty members of a mafia gang based in Corleone, Sicily. In the foreground, their boss, Luciano Liggio, talks to his lawyer. The Sicilian mafia are heavily involved in the drugs trade.*

case study · case study · case study · case study · case study

Canadian businessman, Doug Steele, owns a nightclub in Moscow called the Hungry Duck. He thinks he has already paid out £625,000 in bribes to the Russian mafia and the Moscow police. He has also survived being kidnapped by the mafia. Doug says, 'You have to grease the palm or you won't be in business.' The Russian government estimates that the Russian mafia controls 40 per cent of private business and 60 per cent of state-owned companies. Unofficial sources claim that 80 per cent of Russian banks are controlled directly or indirectly by criminals. According to Doug, 'If it was not for the mafia there would not be an economy. They are a major driving force behind what goes on here.'

The drugs trade

Since the 1930s, the smuggling and selling of drugs has been the major activity of organized crime. The drugs trade has expanded in recent years due to greater economic freedom and the opening up of new markets, such as in Russia and Eastern Europe. The United Nations estimates that there are more than fifty million regular users of hard drugs (heroin and cocaine, for example) around the world. The global trade may be worth as much as 400 billion dollars a year, creating employment for tens of thousands of people.

Many drug dealers operate just as individuals or in small, loose-knit groups. But others organize themselves into international gangs, which sell drugs in much the same way that ordinary businesses sell their products, raising and lowering prices according to the level of demand, and exploring new ways of increasing their profits.

▼ *A police anti-drugs unit attacks poppy fields in Colombia. These fields belong to criminal gangs who produce heroin from the poppies. The Colombian government regularly sprays herbicides (plant poisons) on fields growing poppies as part of its war on drugs.*

▶ *Governments try to stop the drugs trade by searching people and vehicles for drugs as they enter the country. Here a shipment of cocaine has been seized in Miami, USA.*

For example, in the early 1990s, Colombian gangs wanted to gain a foothold in the Puerto Rican drugs market, so they began supplying heroin samples free to potential users. By 2000, Puerto Rico had a large population of heroin addicts.

Much of the world's heroin is produced in Afghanistan. From there it is transported west into western Asia, before finally arriving on the streets of European cities. Cocaine also has a long journey to make from South America to the USA, Africa and Europe. This has been a problem for drug smugglers, who risk being caught at national borders. A cheaper and less dangerous alternative for drug producers and dealers is to trade in chemical drugs, such as ecstasy, which can be produced in Europe or the United States.

"
'The abuse of heroin among youth is a serious problem. Children as young as 13 have been found involved in heroin abuse. According to statistics in 1999, heroin overdose has caused more deaths than traffic accidents.'
Interpol (the International Police Organization)
"

4.What are political crimes?

Fighting the system

People sometimes commit crimes because of their political beliefs, for example if they think a law is unfair. In a democracy it is legal to campaign against the government or against its policies, unless demonstrators use violence.

In most countries, before the twentieth century women could not vote in elections. A women's movement, known as the Suffragettes, began in Britain in the early twentieth century, determined to change this law. Women chained themselves to railings, poured acid in ballot boxes (where votes were collected), burned letters in post boxes, and broke shop windows. They committed these crimes in order to attract publicity to their cause. The strategy eventually worked, and British women over the age of 21 were given the vote in 1928.

Another example of people breaking the law for their political beliefs occurred in America in the 1950s and 1960s. For most of the twentieth century, African Americans in the southern USA faced discrimination every day.

▼ In March 1960, several thousand black residents of the South African township of Sharpeville decided to break the apartheid laws by leaving their passes at home (all black people had to carry passes) and demonstrating against the unfair system. Police opened fire on the demonstration killing 67 protesters and injuring 180.

They were kept apart from white people in buses, schools, parks and libraries, and were frequently attacked by racists. Many were prevented from voting in elections.

A movement began in the 1950s demanding civil rights for black people. Protesters broke the segregation laws by sitting in white-only areas of buses and restaurants. The civil rights movement deliberately flouted unfair laws. As a result of its campaigns, the law was changed. By 1966, black people throughout America were given political and social equality.

▲ *An anti-war demonstration in Los Angeles, USA, on 6 October 2002. In democratic countries, peaceful protests against government policy are legal.*

case study · case study · case study · case study · case study

Steve Biko was a campaigner against the apartheid system in South Africa. 'Apartheid' is an Afrikaans word meaning 'separateness'. Under this system, the black population were not able to vote, they were not allowed to live on or own land except in areas set aside for them, and they were kept rigidly segregated from white people. In 1969, Biko formed an organization to help black people get legal aid and medical care. He was arrested several times between 1975 and 1977, because of his activities. In September 1977 he was beaten up so badly while being interrogated by police that he died from brain damage. The brutal nature of his death led to an international outcry, and Biko became a symbol of black resistance to the apartheid regime. In 1994, under sustained pressure, the apartheid system finally collapsed, and black South Africans were given their freedom.

Terrorism

weblinks

For more information about different types of terrorism, go to www.waylinks.co.uk/series/why/crime

Some people are prepared to kill or maim civilians in order to put pressure on a government to change its policies. They are called terrorists. To achieve their aims, they may explode bombs in crowded areas, kill selected individuals, kidnap people or hijack planes, often as part of a carefully organized campaign. Terrorists do not see themselves as criminals or murderers, but as soldiers in a war against enemy governments. This is how they justify their violence.

Terrorists act this way for different reasons. Some want to change society politically. For example, between the 1960s and 1980s, many terrorist groups believed that the world's richer countries were dominated by businesses which exploited their workers, and kept the rest of the world in poverty. These groups argued that the governments of the richer countries supported this system, and they were determined to overthrow them.

Other terrorist groups are driven by a desire to create their own homeland or to win political freedom for their people. The Palestine Liberation Organization wants to form an independent nation of Palestine on territory now controlled by Israel. Another terrorist group, the Kurdish Worker's Party, aims to establish a country for the Kurdish people in an area presently part of Turkey.

▲ *Journalists gather around the scene of a car bomb attack in Bilbao, Spain. The attack was blamed on the terrorist group ETA, who are fighting for an independent Basque state.*

▲ Ground Zero: the site of the collapsed World Trade Center in New York. The building was targeted by terrorists on 11 September 2001.

Since the 1980s there has been a rise in religiously motivated terrorism, particularly in the Islamic world. Islamic terrorists believe they are fighting a holy war against the enemies of Islam. The main targets of their attacks have been Israel and the USA. They are opposed to Israel's control of land that formerly belonged to Palestinians (most of whom are Muslim), and condemn American support for Israel.

FACT:
The world's worst terrorist attack occurred in September 2001. Over three thousand people were killed when two passenger aeroplanes were deliberately flown into the twin towers in New York City, causing them to collapse. A third aircraft was flown into the Pentagon - the US Defense Department headquarters in Washington D.C. - and a fourth hijacked plane crash-landed in Pennsylvania. The terrorist group responsible was Al Qaeda, an extreme Islamic group dedicated to the destruction of the USA.

5. What methods do the police use?

The history of policing

A police force is an organization responsible for maintaining public order and safety, and enforcing the law. The main job of the police is to prevent and detect crime. Forms of policing have existed for several thousand years. Early police forces, such as the cohorts who kept order in ancient Rome, were usually part of the military. A military police force also existed in seventeenth-century Japan, where the chief of police of each castle town was a sword-carrying samurai warrior.

Until the nineteenth century, there was no police force in England and Wales. If a crime was committed, citizens would band together to hunt down the criminal. Constables and watchmen would guard the cities at night, but the investigation and solving of crimes was left up to the victims. They often hired bounty-hunters who, for a reward, would try to capture criminals and return stolen property to its owner. This system also operated in Australia, Canada and the USA in the early nineteenth century. By contrast, a well-organized police force was established in France by the eighteenth century.

weblinks

For more information about international crime and Interpol, go to www.waylinks.co.uk/ series/why/crime

▼ *Police arrest a suffragette in Hyde Park, London, in 1914. In the early twentieth century, police uniforms, with their tall helmets, were deliberately designed to make policemen appear big and imposing.*

Faced with rising crime rates, a police force was finally established in London in 1829, and in the rest of England by 1856. American cities began establishing police departments in the mid-nineteenth century. In the early 1900s state police forces were created to deal with crime in rural areas, and a national police force, the Federal Bureau of Investigation (FBI), to investigate national crimes.

During the twentieth century, police forces in Europe and North America became increasingly efficient at reaching crime scenes early. They were helped by the introduction of national emergency telephone numbers, police cars and radios, and later by street cameras.

FACT:
The International Criminal Police Organization (Interpol) was founded in 1923 and has its headquarters in Paris, France. There are currently 177 member states. Each member state has its own Interpol office. These offices are responsible for passing on information about criminals that may be of interest to other countries, and for carrying out enquiries or arrests on behalf of other countries.

 A police officer in Austin, Texas, hands out anti-drug literature to children. Since the 1980s, great efforts have been made in Britain and the United States to bring the police closer to the communities they work in.

Methods of detection

Finding people who had committed crimes was not at first the main aim of the English and American police forces. Their job was to prevent crimes from taking place. However, as crime rates continued to rise, the police were asked to take responsibility for the investigation of crimes, and detective departments were set up.

weblinks

For more information about police technology and forensic science, go to www.waylinks.co.uk/series/why/crime

Developments in forensic science, which is the study of clues at a crime scene or found on a victim, helped detectives in their investigations. In the nineteenth century, it was discovered that everyone has a unique set of fingerprints. During the 1880s, ways of recording inked impressions of fingerprints were developed. The first identification of a criminal by the use of fingerprints was in Argentina in 1892. By the early 1900s, fingerprinting had become an established part of police procedure in many countries.

▼ *A murder scene is examined in Paris, Texas, in 1893. In the nineteenth century, police had few of the techniques available today. They had no way of identifying the blood of a murder victim, or even of knowing whether blood was human or animal.*

A detective at the forensic science laboratory in Syracuse, New York, examines a fingerprint on a metal cap. Under laser light, the prints show up in greater detail.

In the 1920s, forensic scientists discovered methods of comparing bullets, so helping police to identify the murder weapon in a shooting. In the 1930s, techniques were invented for identifying blood types and recognizing voices. Libraries of typical facial features were established to help in the visual identification of criminals. Drawings of features could be fitted together to create a likeness of a suspect based on the description of a witness.

Today, many forensic techniques have been enhanced by computer power. This has greatly reduced the time needed to do many tasks, such as identification of fingerprints, faces, voices, or bullets. Advanced cameras are now used to photograph crime scenes and beam pictures to specialists for analysis. As a result of these advances, experts can pinpoint exact times and causes of death in most murders.

FACT:
In 1987, a new method of establishing guilt or innocence was used for the first time: DNA profiling. DNA (deoxyribonucleic acid) is the part of our body's cells that determines our characteristics, and is unique to each of us. Criminals can take steps to avoid leaving fingerprints at a crime scene, but it is very difficult not to leave any physical traces, such as hair or flakes of skin. These traces can be used to identify a person from a DNA analysis.

6. How does the justice system work?

Arrest and trial

In most democratic countries, a person can be arrested if a police officer suspects that he or she has committed a crime. Arresting someone means taking them to a police station and holding them there, to be charged with an offence or to be brought before a court.

▲ *A protester being arrested by British police at a demonstration against cruelty to animals.*

This is known as being taken into police custody. Suspects remain in custody until a court deals with their charges. Once they are in the justice system, they are known as 'defendants'.

Under a democratic system, defendants are regarded as innocent until they are proved guilty. They normally have the following rights:
• The right to remain silent. They do not have to answer questions that may make them appear guilty.
• To be brought before court within a reasonable time.
• To have a lawyer to defend their rights and argue their case in court.

weblinks▸

For more information about criminal justice systems, go to www.waylinks.co.uk/series/why/crime

Most English-speaking countries use trial by jury for serious crimes. The jury is usually made up of twelve citizens who are presented with the facts of the case. They must then decide in private on the guilt or innocence of the defendant. If their verdict (judgement) is guilty, the judge decides on the sentence (punishment). In other countries, such as France, Germany and the Netherlands, there is no jury. The judge, or a panel of judges, decide on both the verdict and the sentence.

▶ *Defendants are provided with a lawyer who argues their case in court. Another lawyer argues the case for the prosecution.*

case study · case study · case study · case study · case study

In non-democratic countries, like Iraq when it was under Saddam Hussein's rule, the justice system is controlled by the government, and the rights of defendants are not generally respected. There is no right to a lawyer. Abd al-Wahad al-Rifa'i was a retired 56-year-old schoolteacher living in Baghdad. One day, the police came to his house and placed him under arrest. They were suspicious of al-Rifa'i because his brother, who lived abroad, was a member of an opposition movement, and they believed that the two men had been in contact. Al-Rifa'i was held in prison for over two years without being charged or tried. In March 2002, he was executed by hanging. When his family collected his body, they saw that it bore the marks of torture.

Is the justice system fair?

Do defendants always get fairly treated? In democratic countries there are safeguards to protect a defendant's rights. For example, a person cannot be arrested unless a police officer has evidence that the person has committed, or is about to commit, a crime. However, the system can be abused. During the 1970s and 1980s, young black people in English cities were frequently arrested with no evidence of wrongdoing.

If arresting officers do not read a suspect his or her rights, or if they use undue force during interrogation, any evidence they obtain cannot be used in a trial. There are also restrictions on how the police can spy on a suspect or search their property. These activities normally require a warrant, which is a written authorization from a judge. Although these restrictions are sometimes ignored in democratic countries, it is quite rare because civil rights groups and the media keep an eye open for any abuses of the system.

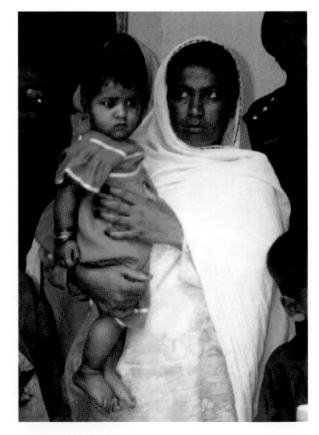

▶ *Zafran Bibi, a Pakistani woman who was accused of adultery, and sentenced to death by stoning by an Islamic court in 2000. The sentence was overturned in 2002.*

◄ *Jury members being sworn in for the trial of the black former sports star, O.J. Simpson. Jury members are deliberately selected from different ethnic backgrounds to avoid any suspicion of racial bias.*

In non-democratic countries, it is often the case that people are arrested on suspicion of a crime, with no evidence of wrongdoing required to support the arrest. They are sometimes mistreated during questioning, and can often be spied on or have their property searched without a warrant.

In countries that employ a jury system, care is generally taken over the selection of the jury to avoid possible bias. For example, in a case involving a racist incident, the jury will be chosen to include people from different ethnic backgrounds.

66

'The public's interest in courtroom proceedings isn't idle curiosity. Taxpayers contribute significant amounts of money to support the state's criminal justice system. They have a right to know how well that system is working. The public shouldn't have to rely on blind faith that the criminal justice system is serving its interests well and protecting the rights of the state and the defendant.'

Orlando Sentinel, *Editorial: A Wise Ruling, 16 October 2002*

99

Trial by media

Newspapers and TV are attracted to criminal trials and major murder cases, especially those involving celebrities. Sometimes their involvement can threaten the course of justice. For example, the media can sometimes put extreme pressure on the police and the courts to make an arrest or obtain a conviction. This can endanger the rights of defendants. When Mozambican journalist Carlos Cardoso was murdered in 2000, the crime investigation was heavily criticized by the media. It is generally believed that the eventual arrest of several suspects was mostly because of pressure exerted by local newspapers.

▼ *Timothy McVeigh – the man responsible for the deaths of 168 people in the Oklahoma City bombing – on trial in 1996. Before the trial began, the publicity surrounding this case was so huge that the judge decided to move it to another city in order to make sure that McVeigh got a fair trial.*

In countries like Australia, Canada and Britain, there are restrictions on the way the media can report a crime before and during a trial. They can only report what is said in court, and are not allowed to interview participants in the trial. This is because there is a danger that judges or juries may form an idea of the guilt or innocence of the defendant before hearing the evidence in court.

In the USA no such law exists, and the media are free to report on a trial as they choose. This can lead to problems. For example, during the O.J. Simpson trial, when a famous American footballer and film actor was accused of murdering his wife, there was so much pre-trial publicity, it proved very difficult to find a jury which could be regarded as unbiased. Some countries, such as the USA, allow cameras to televise certain trials. It is argued that the public has a right to know what goes on in a courtroom. However, it is possible that cameras may affect the way people behave in court, and even influence the outcome of the trial.

▼ *Louise Woodward was accused of killing twenty-one-month old Matthew Eapen while he was in her care. The trial attracted enormous press attention in the United States and in Great Britain.*

"'I would hate to see it go the way [in Britain] it has in the US…. These are people's lives you're dealing with – this is not a soap opera … do you really want the public to be policing the courtroom and making those decisions instead of the twelve people [the jury]? You may as well have an opinion poll on TV?'

Louise Woodward, the first British woman to be involved in a televised trial, 1997. She was a British nanny working in the USA who was accused of killing the baby left in her care

7. How are offenders punished?

The history of punishment

Punishments in the ancient world tended to be very harsh. In ancient Babylon, people who killed, told lies about others, stole temple property, or mixed with other criminals received the death penalty. They could be drowned, stoned, hanged or beheaded.

The death penalty was also common in ancient Rome, and the form of execution depended on the guilty person's social status. Important people were either banished or beheaded. Ordinary people were hanged, burned, buried in mines or torn apart by wild animals in an arena for public entertainment.

▲ *Ancient Roman punishments could be very harsh, as can be seen from this third-century mosaic from Tunisia.*

" Tacitus, the Roman historian, tells us about the punishments for various crimes amongst the Iron-Age tribes in Germany: 'The mode of execution varies according to the offence. Traitors and deserters are hanged in trees: cowards, shirkers ... are pressed down under a wicker hurdle into the slimy mud of a bog ... offenders against the state should be made a public example of, whereas deeds of shame should be buried out of men's sight.'
Tacitus, The Germania "

In Europe in the early Middle Ages (AD 400–1100) the punishment of thieves and murderers was left to the family of the victim. This was gradually replaced by a system in which the criminal paid a fine to the victim or their family depending on the severity of the crime. By the 1100s people began to believe that serious crimes, such as robbery and murder, were not merely a matter for the victim, but were a crime against society as a whole.

In the fifteenth and sixteenth centuries, religious divisions in Europe led to many executions for heresy (holding beliefs that go against the established faith) and treason. Punishments included burning at a stake, hanging and beheading.

By the eighteenth century, the most common form of execution was hanging in Britain and America, and beheading in France. Other punishments from this period included transportation to colonies such as Australia (for British prisoners), pressing to death (in which weights were piled on the guilty person's chest), and flogging.

weblinks

For more information about the history of crime and punishment, go to www.waylinks.co.uk/ series/why/crime

Prisons

Today, imprisonment is the major form of punishment for serious crimes. Prison life is not intended to be easy. Prisoners are confined for much of the day in locked cells; they face loneliness and boredom; they don't have access to the goods and services of the outside world; and they can only meet their families and friends at set times and always under supervision. Prisons have three main purposes: to punish criminals, to reform criminals, and to keep people safe by preventing criminals from being out on the street.

weblinks

For more information about prisons, go to
www.waylinks.co.uk/
series/why/crime

Isolating offenders from the rest of society in prisons is a convenient solution to the problem of crime. However, this has led to the problem of prison overcrowding. The world's prison population in 2000 was between eight and ten million, two million of whom were in the USA. Another growing problem is violence between prisoners. In Colombia, for example, 1,200 inmates were killed by their fellow prisoners between 1991 and 2001. Inmate murders are also common in Brazil, Kenya and Venezuela.

▼ *Hostages held during a 2001 prison uprising in São Paulo, Brazil, are released. The twenty-five hour riot left twelve people dead.*

Prisons are often harsh, unfriendly places. Most inmates have little opportunity for work, training, education or counselling.

Do prisons work? They keep dangerous criminals off the streets. However, they rarely succeed in reforming people. Former prisoners often commit crimes again when they come out, and prisons can even act as 'crime schools' where inmates can learn new tricks of the trade.

Prisons are also very expensive, which is why governments are increasingly turning to other forms of punishment for lesser offences. These include probation, in which offenders are kept under regular supervision, and fines. Community service, where offenders are sentenced to a certain number of hours of work in their local community, is another alternative to prison. Some police forces have experimented with electronic tagging, in which a tracking device is attached to the offender's body, so that police can know where he or she is. Tagged offenders usually have to stay at home at certain times of the day and throughout the night.

FACT:
Overcrowding and disease are particular problems in Russia, which had over a million prisoners in 2000. Approximately one out of every ten inmates is infected with tuberculosis (TB), a bacterial disease. High rates of TB have also been reported in the prisons of Brazil and India.
Human Rights Watch

Capital punishment

Capital punishment is the legal killing of a human being – the severest punishment of all. Because of changing attitudes to crime and punishment, over half the countries in the world have now abolished the death penalty. In 2001, 84 countries continued to use the death penalty. They included India, Japan and the USA.

Some of those who oppose capital punishment see it as an immoral punishment. They believe that no criminal deserves to be killed, even those who have killed others. Others argue that innocent people may be executed, and that the death penalty is given more often to blacks than to whites.

weblinks

For more information about campaigns against the death penalty, go to www.waylinks.co.uk/series/why/crime

'The death penalty is not used enough. The simple fact remains that there are way too many murders a year. I believe the murder rate can and will be lowered if the death penalty was a real threat for these criminals.... Too many times criminals sit on death row for years wasting away, waiting to die. What type of life is that? Why not put these people out of their misery and save the taxpayers money?'

Billy Foulds, Texas, a pro-death penalty campaigner, writing in 2001

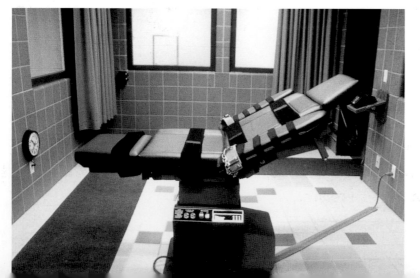

◀ *The chair in which Timothy McVeigh was executed by lethal injection in June 2001. Ten of the survivors of the building he bombed in Oklahoma City witnessed his death.*

Between 1973 and 2001, 102 prisoners were released from death row in the USA after evidence emerged of their innocence of the crimes for which they were sentenced to death. Other US prisoners have gone to their deaths despite serious doubts over their guilt.

Those in favour of the death penalty claim it deters others from committing murder. However, opponents argue that since most murders are not planned in advance, few people will be thinking of punishment when they murder someone. Also, crime rates have not noticeably risen in countries which have abolished the death penalty. In some cases they have fallen. In Canada, where capital punishment was abolished in 1976, the murder rate (per 100,000) fell from 3.09 in 1975 to 1.76 in 1999.

There are other arguments in favour of the death penalty:
• Murderers who do not serve life sentences sometimes kill again once released.
• Keeping a person in prison for many years costs taxpayers a lot of money.
• If the majority of the population are in favour of the death penalty, it is undemocratic to abolish it.
• It is a way of avenging the death of murder victims.

In the USA people are executed either by lethal injection or the electric chair. In strict Islamic countries, such as Saudi Arabia and Iran, people are sometimes beheaded or stoned to death.

▲ In December 2001 the death sentence against Mumia Abu-Jamal (above) was overturned. His case was championed by death-penalty opponents.

'The death penalty is disgusting, particularly if it condemns an innocent. But it remains an injustice even when it falls on someone who is guilty of a crime.'
Giuliano Amato,
Prime Minister of Italy,
14 September 2000,
commenting on a scheduled execution in Virginia, USA

Children and the law

In the past, child criminals were often given the same punishments as adults. At the end of the nineteenth century, children began to get their own courts and sentencing was changed to take their youth into account. Correctional schools for young people were set up in countries such as Britain. These were harsh places with strict discipline. Attitudes have now changed, and efforts have been made to try to reform children, rather than simply punish them.

In 1985, the United Nations agreed on a set of minimum standards of justice for people under eighteen years old, known as the Beijing Rules. Member states who signed up to the rules agreed to the following:

• No child offender should be tortured, beaten, executed or sentenced to life imprisonment without possibility of future release.

• The arrest, detention and imprisonment of a child should be a done as a matter of last resort, and for the shortest appropriate period of time.

• Imprisoned children should be separated from adults, and should have the right to maintain contact with their family if appropriate.

▲ *These Colombian children who live on the street have little or no chance of finding legitimate jobs. They are quite likely to get drawn into crime, or be recruited by a drug gang.*

weblinks

For more information about justice for young people around the world, go to www.waylinks.co.uk/series/why/crime

In the years since the signing of the Beijing Rules, many countries have introduced laws to protect young offenders, although widespread human rights abuses still remain. Many children are denied their legal rights, are held in poor conditions, and suffer violence at the hands of guards and police. Some who commit murder when young are even put to death, in places like Iran and the USA.

case study · case study · case study · case study · case study

In February 1993 Jon Venables and Robert Thomson, both aged 10, murdered a two-year-old boy named James Bulger. After snatching him in a shopping centre in Liverpool, England, they battered him to death and left his body on a railway line. The case provoked huge public grief, and anger towards Venables and Thomson. After a public trial in an adult court, the boys were sentenced to eight years' imprisonment. The trial was criticized by the European Commission on Human Rights which argued that the boys should have been tried in a youth court. The boys were released in 2001, aged 18. Many members of the British public, including James Bulger's mother, believed they should have served a longer sentence. The boys were given new identities to protect them from revenge attacks.

Caught on security camera, Jamie Bulger is led away to his death.

Turning children away from crime

Crime remains a major concern for people around the world. Traditionally governments have focused on punishing people who have already committed crimes. They spend millions each year on the administration of justice systems, and millions more on imprisoning offenders.

By contrast, very little is spent on attempting to deter people from a life of crime in the first place. Governments in developed countries spend less than one per cent of criminal justice spending on crime prevention. Yet finding effective ways of preventing crime could end up saving governments and taxpayers a lot of money, while also making the world a safer place.

To stop children turning to crime, parents could be given more guidance on the dangers of drugs, or of allowing their children to watch violent programmes on TV.

▼ *There are many reasons why children break the law. They may be led into such actions by a sense of anger or frustration, through peer pressure, or by a desire to 'prove themselves'. Talking over their feelings with a trained professional can help to bring these issues into the open.*

Children who play sport outside school are less likely to turn to crime. A survey by the National Crime Prevention Council found that communities with youth club programmes experienced 13 per cent fewer juvenile crimes.

The parents and teachers of young children who show signs of aggressive behaviour could receive special training. Such children could be counselled and supervised by trained professionals.

A major reason why young people turn to crime is their sense of being excluded from society's benefits. If they were offered more opportunities for training and recreation, then perhaps a life of crime might not seem as attractive. The ultimate goal should be to show young people that they can abide by the law and still lead an enjoyable and rewarding life. Perhaps if more young people felt that way, there would be less crime in the future.

FACT:
One obvious way of attacking crime is to reduce the opportunities for it. The theft of mobile phones reached epidemic proportions in Britain in 2000. About 710,000 were stolen – accounting for a third of all personal thefts. Some manufacturers began introducing 'anti-theft chips' which allow mobile phone users to disable the phones from a remote location. They simply phone up their operator and give them a password, and the phone becomes useless to the thief.

GLOSSARY

Apartheid
The political system operating in South Africa between 1948 and 1994. It separated the different peoples living there, and gave special privileges to whites of European origin.

Bounty-hunter
Someone who pursues wanted criminals for financial reward.

Bribery
The offering of money to persuade somebody to do something, especially something illegal or dishonest.

Burglary
The crime of entering a building without permission to commit a theft.

Civil rights movement
A political movement that sprang up in the USA during the 1960s that demanded equal rights for black Americans.

Cocaine
An illegal addictive drug obtained from the leaves of the coca plant.

Constable
A low-ranking law enforcement officer.

Custody
The state of being detained by the police or other authorities.

Defendant
A person required to answer criminal charges in a court.

Democracy
A system of government in which the leaders have been elected freely and equally by all the citizens, or a country run by such a system.

Detention
Being held in custody by police or government authorities.

Discrimination
Unfair treatment of a group of people because of their race, ethnic group, religion, or some other reason.

Ecstasy
An illegal drug used to stimulate or relax the mind artificially.

Electric chair
A chair used to execute people who have been sentenced to death, by passing a powerful electric charge through their bodies.

Ethnic group
A group of a certain race, or a group that shares the same customs, language and culture.

Flogging
Hitting very hard with a whip, strap or stick.

Forensic science
The scientific study of a crime scene.

Gambling
Playing and betting on games of chance in the hope of winning money.

Hacking
Accessing files held on someone else's computer without their permission or knowledge.

Heresy
The holding of a belief that is different from the code of beliefs laid down by an established religious authority, such as the Church.

Heroin
An illegal addictive drug obtained from morphine. Morphine is obtained from opium poppies.

Hijacking
Taking control of a public transport vehicle, such as an aircraft, taking those on board hostage, and diverting it to another destination.

Immigration
The flow of people into a country to live there.

Interrogation
Questioning someone closely, often in an aggressive way, especially as part of an official investigation.

Intimidation
Persuading somebody to do something by frightening them.

Joyriding
The crime of taking a car without permission and, often, driving it dangerously at high speed.

Jury
A panel of people chosen to decide on the guilt or innocence of a defendant in a court of law.

Juvenile
Young.

Kidnapping
The crime of forcibly taking away and holding someone prisoner. Kidnappers usually ask for money (a ransom) in exchange for the prisoner.

Lawyer
Someone who is professionally qualified to give legal advice and to represent people in a court.

Lethal injection
A form of execution in which deadly poison is introduced into the body of a person by injection.

Libel
A false statement about someone, made in a written or printed form, that damages their reputation.

Loansharking
Lending money at very high rates of interest.

Manslaughter
The unplanned and unintended killing of another person.

Murder
The crime of killing another person deliberately.

Overdose
A dangerously large dose of a drug that may lead to death.

Perjury
Lying to a court while under oath to tell the truth.

Poaching
Hunting animals on other people's land.

Police custody (to be in)
To be held at a police station after having been placed under arrest.

Pornography
Sexually explicit films, magazines, photographs and other materials.

Prohibition
The period between 1920 and 1933 when alcoholic drinks were banned in the USA.

Prostitution
The act of engaging in sex with someone in exchange for money.

Protection racket
An arrangement by which a person or gang demands money from a person or business in return for a guarantee that they will not hurt that person or damage his or her property.

Racism
The belief that people of different races have different qualities and abilities and that some races are superior to others.

Rights
Entitlements, freedoms or privileges granted under law.

Robbery
The crime of taking something from someone else using violence or the threat of violence.

Samurai
A member of a class of warriors who were powerful in Japan between the eleventh and nineteenth centuries.

Segregation
The forced separation of a person or group of people from the rest of a community.

Serial killer
Somebody who murders a number of people over a period of time, often using the same method each time.

Shoplifting
The crime of stealing goods from a shop while pretending to be shopping normally.

Smuggling
Avoiding tax by transporting goods, such as alcohol or cigarettes, into a country in secret.

Stoning
A form of execution in which stones are thrown at someone until they are dead.

Suffragettes
Women who campaigned for the vote in Britain during the early twentieth century.

Terrorism
The use of violence against civilians and political leaders in order to achieve political aims.

Theft
The crime of stealing somebody else's property.

Treason
The crime of betraying one's country or one's sovereign.

Truancy
Absence from school without permission.

Tuberculosis
An infectious disease that usually affects the lungs.

Unbiased
Fair; not swayed by outside influences.

Vandalism
The deliberate damaging or destruction of someone else's property.

Warrant
Official authorization that gives the police special powers, such as the right to search or arrest someone.

Watchman
Somebody employed to guard or patrol an area.

FURTHER INFORMATION

BOOKS TO READ

For children
Citizen's Guide to Law and Order by Paul Wignall (Heinemann Library, 2003)
Crime and Punishment (Moral Dilemmas) by Philip Steele (Evans, 2003)
Crime and Punishment (Twentieth Century Issues) by Alison Brownlie (Hodder Wayland, 1999)
Crime in the Community (In the News) by Iris Teichmann (Franklin Watts, 2002)

For teachers
Crime and Punishment: A Study Across Time by Roger Whiting (Stanley Thornes, 1987)
Crime and Society by Frances Heidenshohn (Macmillan, 1989)
Psychology in Practice: Crime by Julie Harrower (Hodder & Stoughton, 2001)
Textbook on Criminology by Katherine S. Williams (OUP, 2004)

WEBSITES
For websites that are relevant to this book, go to www.waylinks.co.uk/series/why/crime

INDEX